Happy

CW00369509

Certainly not
for my family...

OTHER BOOKS BY
STEVEN APPLEBY:

Normal Sex
MEN - The Truth

A FAMILY TREE

FIRST PUBLISHED IN 1995 as 'MISERABLE FAMILIES'
This paperback edition first published in 1996

BLOOMSBURY PUBLISHING PLC
2 SOHO SQUARE, LONDON W1V 6HB

ISBN 0-7475-2604-4

Printed and bound by the Bath Press
PHOTOGRAPH of Steven Appleby by Pete Bishop

THIS BOOK WOULD NOT HAVE EXISTED WITHOUT:
My family; Pete Bishop; Jonathan Boatfield; Liz Calder;
Jessamy Calkin; Joe Ewart; Malcolm Garrett;
Kasper de Graaf; Matthew Hamilton; Anita Plank;
The Ginger Prince; Nicola Sherring; Howard Trafford;
Noni Ware; Damien Wayling; Janny Kent

SOME OF THESE DRAWINGS HAVE APPEARED IN:
The Guardian; The Sunday Telegraph; Tatler

This book is printed entirely on paper
made from family trees

HAPPY

FAMILIES

by

Steven Appleby

Very rich relative
from deported branch
of the family.

ASSORTED NAMELESS
INDIVIDUALS IN
POSITIONS OF
AUTHORITY.

No!

No!

No!

No.

No.

No!

Driving
examiner.

No!

Bank
manager.

No!

Fiancée.

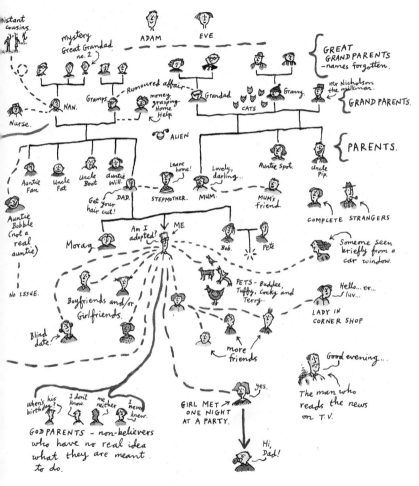

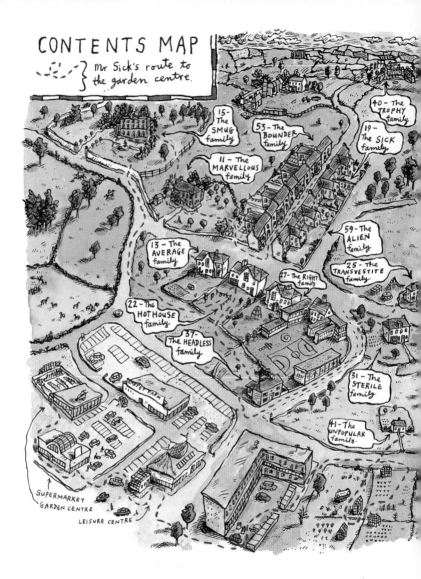

The MARVELLOUS family

RELATIONSHIP CHART

The AVERAGE family

MR ANTHONY AVERAGE
the ANT EXPERT

MRS ANDROID AVERAGE
the ANT EXPERT'S WIFE

MISS POPPET AVERAGE
the ANT EXPERT'S DAUGHTER

MASTER 0.7 AVERAGE
the ANT EXPERT'S SON

the SMUG family

16

In the nursery Nanny Rodent looks after the tiny children from 7:30 am until 7:30 at night.

Mr Smug's three children from his first marriage are visiting for the weekend. He won't see them as they get up after he goes to bed, and vice versa.

What does mummy look like?

I believe in Santa Claus, but not in Daddy.

Brian, Mrs Smug's secretary, answers her letters and invitations.

Foggerty, the maid, clears up the almost archaeological remains of (in order) tea at 3:30 pm; T.V. supper; the adults' bridge evening at 9:00 pm; and the older children's orgy of video watching and chocolate eating.

The airport, Watson, and step on it!

Step on what, mr Smug?

Cook bakes biscuits in the shape of hangmen and their victims. It helps her think.

AN AUTHOR RESEARCHING A BOOK:

The SICK family

PETS CORNER

The HOTHOUSE family

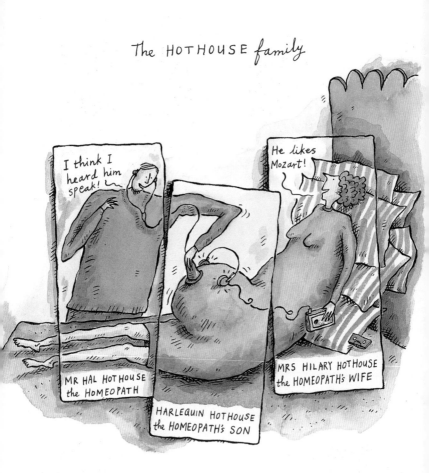

Constructive play fills Harlequin's day.

HARLEQUIN HOTHOUSE ~ A Life...

2 YEARS OLD

10 YEARS OLD

14 YEARS OLD

20 YEARS OLD

26 YEARS OLD

32 YEARS OLD

The TRANSVESTITE family

Here are the children's dolls:

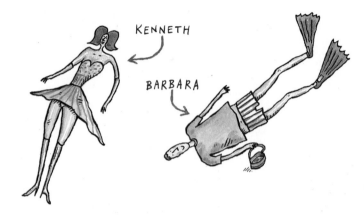

KENNETH

BARBARA

And the family dog and cat:

Miaow!

Woof!
Woof!

The RIGHT family

28

The STERILE family

33

34

The UNFAITHFUL family

MR UTTERLY UNFAITHFUL
the UNDERTAKER

MRS UNBELIEVABLY UNFAITHFUL
the UNDERTAKER'S WIFE

The HEADLESS family

38

The TROPHY family

The UNPOPULAR family

Party-time at Mr Unpopular's house.

RENTED RELATIVES *

43

The SOUR family

Pretty boy! Pretty boy! Pretty boy! Pretty boy!

Pretty boy! Pretty boy!

MISS SOUR the SPINSTER'S BUDGIE WILLIE

MISS SOUR the SPINSTER

MISS SOUR the SPINSTER'S CAT SMOKY

MISS SOUR the SPINSTER'S CAT SOOTY

The BENDER family

The INVISIBLE family

MR INVISIBLE MAN

MRS INVISIBLE MAN

49

Mr Invisible Man at work:

The INCREDIBLY-NICE-BUT-DEEPLY-UNHAPPY-UNDERNEATH *family*

The BOUNDER family

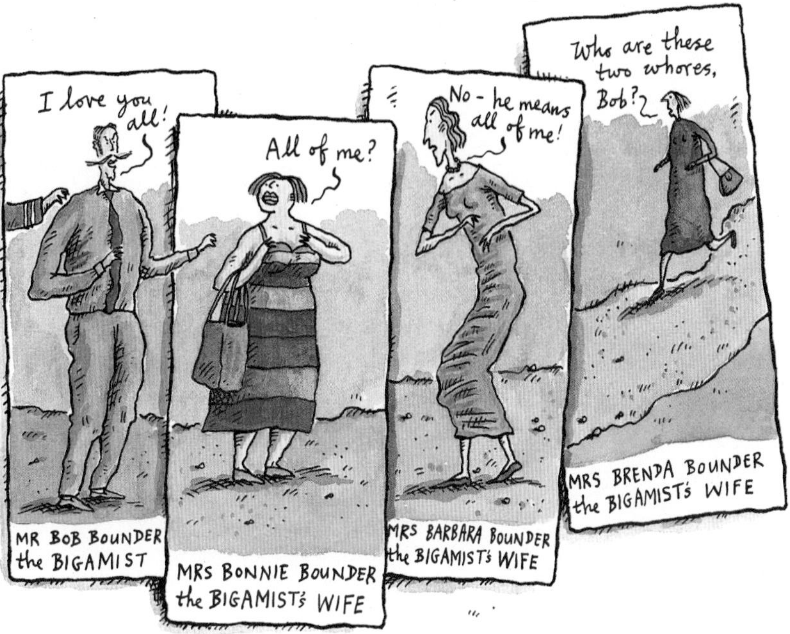

Mr Bounder's brother, Bernard, is an airline pilot and an even more successful bigamist.

The BIAS family

57

The NOBODY family

MR NOBODY

MRS NOBODY

MASTER NOBODY

MISS NOBODY

The ALIEN family

MOVING DAY...

The CYNICAL family

The NORMAL family

The OLD family

The DOORMAT family

The SWOP family

The STEP family

The NUCLEAR family

The HAPPY FAMILY RETIREMENT HOME

The _____ family*

Stick
photos
here.

*Insert your own family name in the space provided.

The EXIT family

A pruned family tree

THREATS
to family life

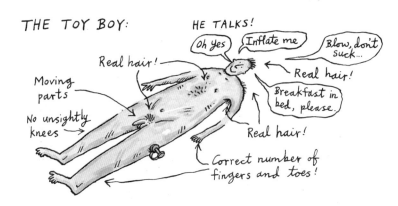

THE TOY GIRL:

THE AU PAIR:

81

THE MILKMAN:

THE POSTMAN:

82

THE LODGER, or RENT BOY:

HERMAN the HERMAPHRODITE:

CHILDREN:

THE CHILD SNATCHER:

85

NOT ENOUGH HOURS IN THE DAY:

A momentary magical window of opportunity opens up between the children going to bed and the onset of complete physical exhaustion.

THE SEVEN-YEAR ITCH:

THE FORTY-YEAR ITCH:

THE AFFAIR!

ACCUSATION:

LOSS OF TRUST:

LACK OF RESPECT:

CRAWLING SKIN:

Don't touch me! You make my skin crawl, going on about tea! You... you... philanderer!

I'll make a fresh pot.

INABILITY TO SLEEP:

I've drunk too much tea.

Me too.

RECONCILIATION:

TEAS MAID

Zzzzzzz

Zzzzzzzz

Yet More
THREATS TO FAMILY LIFE

TOO-TIRED-TO-THINK:

Darling, I want to talk about us...

zzzzzzzzzz snort... snuffle...

WORKAHOLISM:

DEAD:

A Guide to the
IDENTIFICATION
and care of
FAMILY TREES

Family Tree
Seed

Family Tree
Seedlings

Pull
it up.

A Family Weed

Happy
New
Year!

A Christmas
Family Tree

Gallows Family
Tree

I have
a
small
family.

Bonsai Family
Tree

A Topiary Family Tree Group.

Working out the age of your family by counting the rings in your family tree:

my! We go a long way back!

USEFUL CHAIRS made from family trees:

STEVEN APPLEBY was born in 1956 and will die in _____. He is one insignificant bough somewhere in the middle foliage of a family tree which will grow and grow until the top reaches the Land of Giants, whereupon the world will end and Steven and his relatives will climb up to the Giant's Land singing songs of praise. Once there they will be fattened, slaughtered and baked one by one in a giant oven. Some will be boiled on the hob, others dipped in flour and deep-fried. The Giants will complain bitterly when eating Steven, saying: "There's no meat on't," and, "Pop another'n in." Similar things will happen to YOU on YOUR family tree — but not for a few hundred years yet...

July 23rd 1995

94

THE END